24 HOUR HISTORY

THE ATTACK ON PEARL HARBOR

7 DECEMBER 1941

Nel Yomtov

Raintree

Raintree is an imprint of Capstone Global Library
Limited, a company incorporated in England and Wales
having its registered office at 7 Pilgrim Street, London,
EC4V 6LB – Registered company number: 6695582

www.raintreepublishers.co.uk
myorders@raintreepublishers.co.uk

Text © Capstone Global Library Limited 2014
First published in hardback in 2014
The moral rights of the proprietor have been asserted.

Edited by Adam Miller, Abby Colich, and
    John-Paul Wilkins
Designed by Steve Mead
Original illustrations © Advocate Art 2014
Illustrated by Maurizio Campidelli
Production by Victoria Fitzgerald
Originated by Capstone Global Library Ltd
Printed and bound in China

ISBN 978 1 406 27363 2
18 17 16 15 14
10 9 8 7 6 5 4 3 2 1

A full catalogue record for this book is available from
the British Library.

Acknowledgements
We would like to thank Gerard DeGroot for his
invaluable help in the preparation of this book.

Every effort has been made to contact copyright holders
of material reproduced in this book. Any omissions will
be rectified in subsequent printings if notice is given to
the publisher.

All the internet addresses (URLs) given in this book
were valid at the time of going to press. However, due to
the dynamic nature of the internet, some addresses may
have changed, or sites may have changed or ceased to
exist since publication. While the author and publisher
regret any inconvenience this may cause readers, no
responsibility for any such changes can be accepted by
either the author or the publisher.

CONTENTS

Direct quotations are indicated by a yellow background.

Direct quotations appear on the following pages: 24, 36.

INTRODUCTION: THE ROAD TO WAR

In the 1920s, Japan did not have the oil, gas, or other raw materials to become a world power. Japanese leaders decided to invade other nations to seize these resources. In 1937, Japan invaded China.

In 1939, war broke out in Europe when Germany invaded Poland. As the fighting intensified, British and Russian armies fought to stop the Germans' advance across the continent.

In the United States, President Franklin D. Roosevelt had kept America out of the growing conflict. He stopped all trade with Japan and demanded it pull out of China. The United States and Japan were trying to negotiate peace, but tensions between the two nations grew.

Emperor Hirohito of Japan approved Admiral Isoroku Yamamoto's decision to attack the US fleet at Pearl Harbor on the Hawaiian island of Oahu in the Pacific Ocean.

While the United States was busy rebuilding its navy, Japan would attack other resource-rich countries.

The date for the attack was set for Sunday 7 December.*

*American time. In Japan, the day for the attack fell on 8 December.

American sailors at Pearl Harbor had no idea that the Japanese were heading their way.

THE ENEMY APPROACHES

3.42 A.M.

Sunday 7 December 1941, 3.42 a.m., Hawaiian time.* Just 3.2 kilometres (2 miles) from Pearl Harbor, the US minesweeper *Condor* spots a periscope.

The *Condor* sends a message to the nearby US destroyer, *Ward*.

*Hawaiian time is six hours earlier than the time in Washington DC.

6.00 A.M.

The Japanese fleet is now only 400 kilometres (250 miles) north of the Hawaiian island of Oahu. The fleet is commanded by Vice Admiral Chuichi Nagumo. The prize of the fleet is six aircraft carriers, which carry over 400 attack planes.

Next up are the D3A Vals, dive-bombers that carry a 250-kilogram (550-pound) bomb. Fifty-four Vals take to the air in the first wave.

Ninety B5N Type 97 Kates, bombers that can drop an 800-kilogram (1,760-pound) torpedo or bomb, also participate in the first wave. (See map on page 41 to follow the action.)

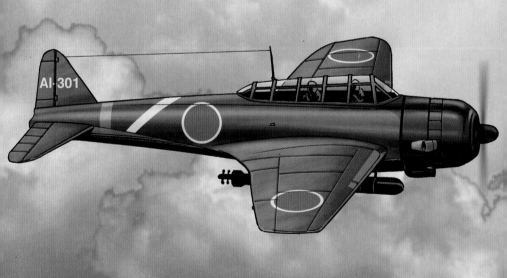

6.26 A.M.

As Japanese pilots turn southwest towards their target, they see the morning sun rise. The vivid shafts of light remind the pilots of the Japanese Rising Sun military flag.

6.45 A.M.

The *Ward* fires depth charges and sinks the Japanese mini-submarine the *Condor* had seen earlier. The submarine is one of five sent to attack Pearl Harbor.

7.51 A.M.

The first wave of attackers splits off into two groups. Zeros strafe PBY Catalina seaplanes, known as flying boats, at Kaneohe Bay Naval Air Station on the island's east coast.

7.53 A.M.

The second group blasts parked aircraft at Ewa Field on the southern coast.

7.55 A.M.

Val dive-bombers drop their loads on Hickam Field. A B-18 Bolo bomber is hit. Twenty-two men are killed. Hangars burst into flames.

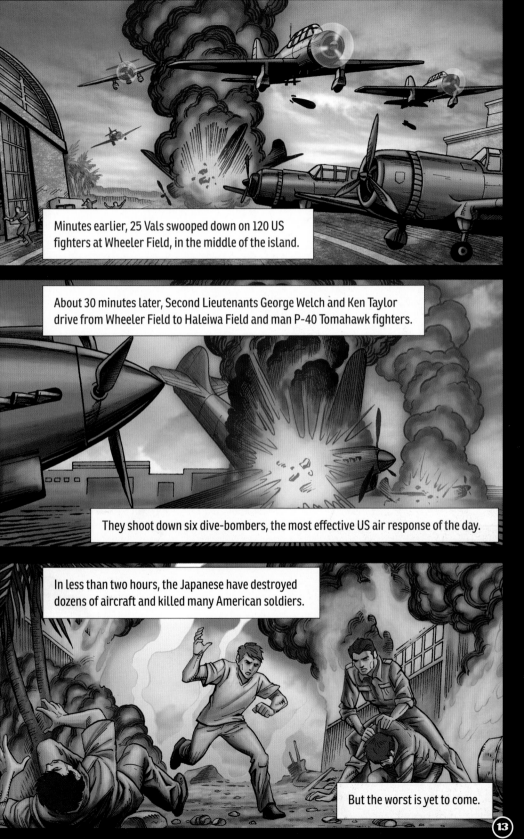

Minutes earlier, 25 Vals swooped down on 120 US fighters at Wheeler Field, in the middle of the island.

About 30 minutes later, Second Lieutenants George Welch and Ken Taylor drive from Wheeler Field to Haleiwa Field and man P-40 Tomahawk fighters.

They shoot down six dive-bombers, the most effective US air response of the day.

In less than two hours, the Japanese have destroyed dozens of aircraft and killed many American soldiers.

But the worst is yet to come.

7.55 A.M.

A torpedo slams into the *Raleigh*, causing it to roll to one side. Other torpedoes strike the light cruiser *Helena* and the minelayer *Oglala* moored next to it.

The attackers strike US vessels moored on the west side of Ford Island in Pearl Harbor.

JAPANESE TORPEDOES AT PEARL HARBOR

A torpedo contains a motor that is attached to a propeller, which spins and moves the torpedo forward. Many US officers believed that Pearl Harbor was safe from torpedo attack because the waters were too shallow for torpedoes to work. The Japanese, however, designed torpedoes especially for use in the shallow harbour. The Type 91 Thunder Fish torpedo was 5.5 metres (18 feet) long and weighed 835 kilograms (1,841 pounds). It could travel 2,000 metres (2,200 yards) at a speed of 77 kilometres (48 miles) per hour. It carried 205 kilograms (452 pounds) of explosives.

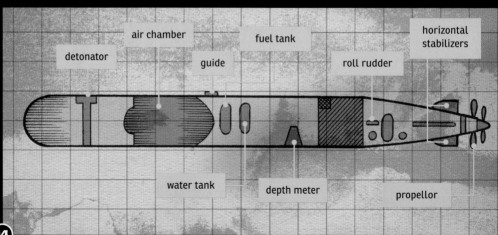

air chamber

fuel tank

horizontal stabilizers

detonator

guide

roll rudder

water tank

depth meter

propellor

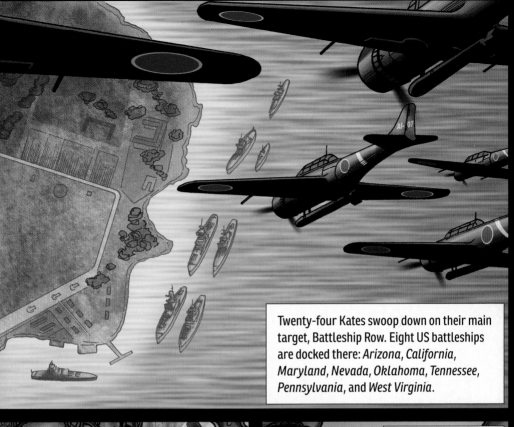

Twenty-four Kates swoop down on their main target, Battleship Row. Eight US battleships are docked there: *Arizona*, *California*, *Maryland*, *Nevada*, *Oklahoma*, *Tennessee*, *Pennsylvania*, and *West Virginia*.

7.58 A.M.

Excellent! A direct hit!

Torpedoes explode into the *West Virginia* and *Oklahoma*.

Shaken by the furious blast, sailors on the *West Virginia* rush to man their battle stations.

Lieutenant Commander Logan Ramsey rushes to a radio room on Ford Island to warn of the attack.

Air raid, Pearl Harbor. This is not a drill! This is not a drill!

As the bombs fall, Yeoman Leonard Webb hastily rushes his wife and child to their car.

Hurry! Hurry! Get yourselves to safety!

8.00 A.M.

The *Oklahoma* is hit again and again, and it begins to roll to one side.

Two torpedoes rip into the side of the *California*. The ship sinks to the bottom of the harbour.

Sailors dive into the oil-slickened, fiery waters. More than 400 are killed.

8.05 A.M.

Men aboard the *Nevada* rush to their battle stations and open fire, shooting down two attackers. Moments later, a torpedo slams into the *Nevada*, ripping a 14 x 9-metre (45 x 30-foot) gash in her bow.

8.05 A.M.

A squadron of 49 Kates targets the *Arizona*, *Tennessee*, and *Maryland*. Each Kate is carrying an 800-kilogram (1,760-pound) armour-piercing bomb.

8.06 A.M. A bomb penetrates the forward magazine of the *Arizona*, where the ship's ammunition is stored.

The vessel erupts in a massive fireball, killing 1,200 men. The *Vestal*, moored next to the *Arizona*, is also damaged in the blast.

8.06 A.M. Two bombs savagely strike the *West Virginia*, which had earlier been damaged by torpedoes. Captain Mervyn Bennion is badly wounded by shrapnel.

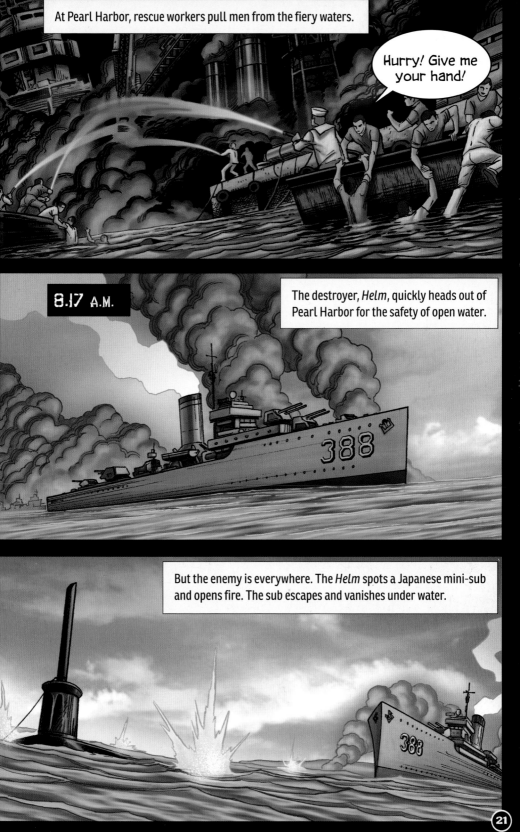

At Pearl Harbor, rescue workers pull men from the fiery waters.

Hurry! Give me your hand!

8.17 A.M.

The destroyer, *Helm*, quickly heads out of Pearl Harbor for the safety of open water.

388

But the enemy is everywhere. The *Helm* spots a Japanese mini-sub and opens fire. The sub escapes and vanishes under water.

388

Got 'im!

Keep firing, Steve!

At Schofield Barracks, Second Lieutenant Stephen Saltzman and Sergeant Lowell Klatt open fire on an attacking Val. As the plane tries to avoid power cables, the men score hits and bring it down.

Meanwhile, at Hickam Field, Japanese planes attack firefighters trying to put out the blazes. Three firefighters are killed.

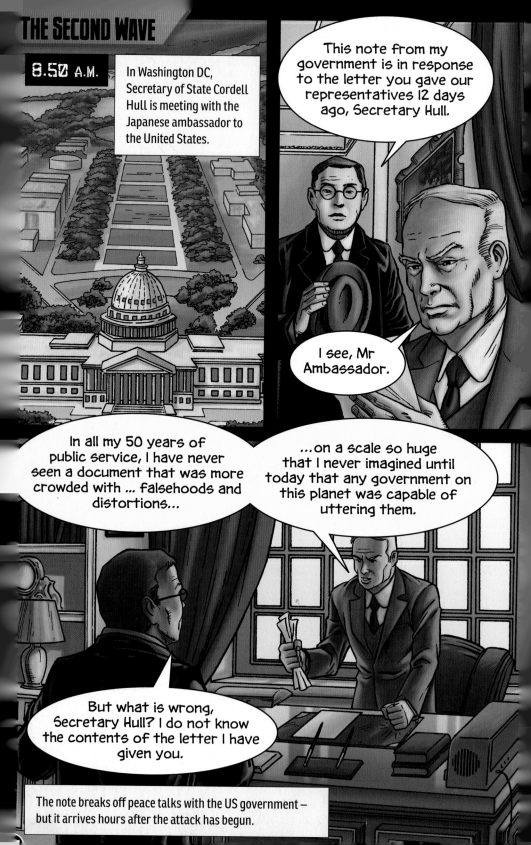

PEACE TALKS

Months before the attack, the United States and Japan began peace talks to settle their differences over Japanese aggression in China. Many attempts failed. On 7 December, Admiral Kichisaburo Nomura, the Japanese ambassador to the United States, was told he would get a message from the Japanese embassy that he was to deliver to Secretary of State Hull by 1.00 p.m. Washington DC time (7.00 a.m. Hawaiian time). In this message, Japan would declare an end to the peace talks. The message, however, was not delivered until almost 3.00 p.m. – long after the attack had begun.

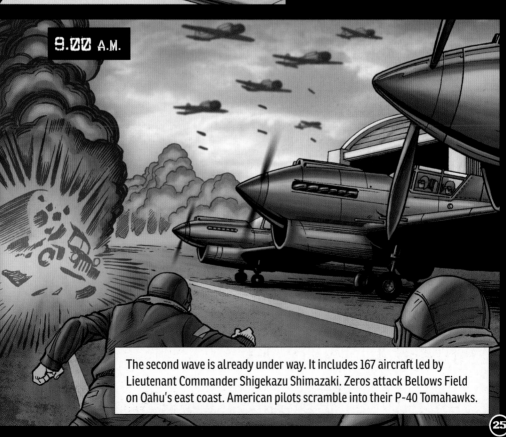

9.00 A.M.

The second wave is already under way. It includes 167 aircraft led by Lieutenant Commander Shigekazu Shimazaki. Zeros attack Bellows Field on Oahu's east coast. American pilots scramble into their P-40 Tomahawks.

Lieutenant George Whiteman begins to lift off the runway but is hit by a burst of enemy gunfire. His plane is thrown out of control and crashes. Whiteman later dies from his injuries.

Lieutenant Sam Bishop gets airborne, but a Zero quickly shoots him down. Bishop is shot in the leg but manages to swim to shore.

9.05 A.M.

Zeros and Vals strafe Wheeler Field in an attack that lasts for nearly 30 minutes. They target parked planes, barracks, a service building, and even a baseball field.

9.05 A.M.

Kaneohe Bay Naval Air Station had already suffered heavy damage in the first wave. Now, 18 Kates drop their loads to finish the job.

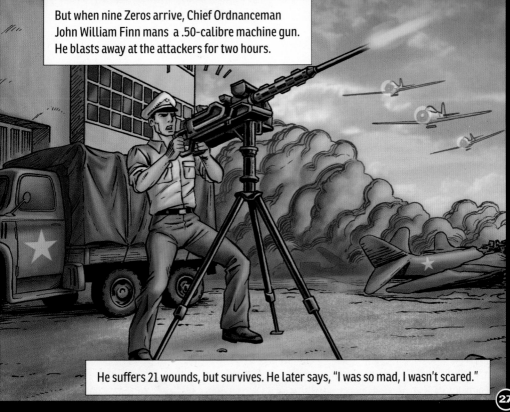

But when nine Zeros arrive, Chief Ordnanceman John William Finn mans a .50-calibre machine gun. He blasts away at the attackers for two hours.

He suffers 21 wounds, but survives. He later says, "I was so mad, I wasn't scared."

9.06 A.M.

At Pearl Harbor, bombs strike the destroyers *Downes* and *Cassin* as they sit in dry dock. Their oil tanks are punctured and they explode in flames. The dry dock is flooded in an attempt to calm the flames, but the rising water lifts the *Cassin* from its blocks and it rolls onto the *Downes*.

The *Pennsylvania*, *Honolulu*, *Raleigh*, *Oglala*, and *Helena* are sinking or barely upright.

9.30 A.M.

Three 250-kilogram (550-pound) bombs hit the destroyer *Shaw*, which is moored in dry dock. The explosions set off raging fires that ignite the *Shaw*'s ammunition store and blow off the entire front part of the ship.

9.37 A.M.

The light cruiser *St Louis* races out of the harbour to the safety of the open seas. Certain it will be spotted and attacked by Japanese aircraft, the *St Louis* quickly ploughs through a cable blocking its way.

9.50 A.M.

The destroyer *Blue* picks up the signal of a mini-sub on its radar. It drops six depth charges and destroys the sub. Minutes later, the *Blue* reportedly sinks another sub that is thought to be chasing the *St Louis*.

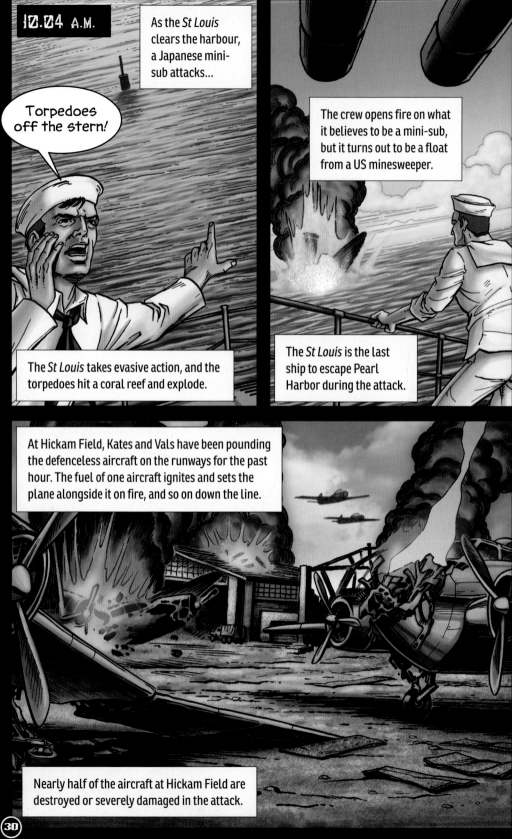

10.04 A.M.

As the *St Louis* clears the harbour, a Japanese mini-sub attacks...

Torpedoes off the stern!

The crew opens fire on what it believes to be a mini-sub, but it turns out to be a float from a US minesweeper.

The *St Louis* takes evasive action, and the torpedoes hit a coral reef and explode.

The *St Louis* is the last ship to escape Pearl Harbor during the attack.

At Hickam Field, Kates and Vals have been pounding the defenceless aircraft on the runways for the past hour. The fuel of one aircraft ignites and sets the plane alongside it on fire, and so on down the line.

Nearly half of the aircraft at Hickam Field are destroyed or severely damaged in the attack.

Commander Fuchida flies over the island to assess the extent of the damage. An earlier report from one of the Japanese pilots seemed to be accurate. It simply said, "Inflicted much damage."

THE LOSSES AT PEARL HARBOR

US military personnel losses were heavy. Deaths totalled 2,335, with 1,143 wounded. Sixty-eight civilians died and another 35 were wounded. Of the ships in the harbour, 18 were either sunk or damaged. The sunken ships were the battleships *Arizona*, *Oklahoma*, *California*, *West Virginia*, the minelayer *Oglala*, and the training ship *Utah*. The United States lost 169 aircraft. In comparison, Japanese losses were low. Just 29 planes were lost and 55 pilots were killed.

12.30 P.M.

Japanese Embassy, Honolulu, Hawaiii

Police and FBI agents burst in and find Japanese officials burning codebooks. They also discover an envelope filled with papers. However, the Americans don't yet know which of the documents are important.

1.00 P.M.

Commander Fuchida returns to his carrier, the *Akagi*, and delivers his report to Vice Admiral Nagumo. Convinced that the first two waves were successful, Nagumo decides not to launch a third wave of attackers.

We've done well enough, Commander. It's time to withdraw.

Nagumo fears the Americans would now be prepared to mount a strong defence against his planes. His greatest concern, however, is a counterstrike from the US carriers.

WHERE WERE THE US AIRCRAFT CARRIERS?

The US Navy's three valuable aircraft carriers – which normally would have been stationed at Pearl Harbor – escaped destruction on 7 December. On 5 December, the *Lexington* was sent to Midway Island in case of a Japanese attack there. The *Enterprise* was at sea and returning to Oahu on 7 December. The *Saratoga* was at the US naval base in San Diego, California, when the attack started. In the months after the attack, the carriers would inflict heavy damage upon the Japanese.

1.12 P.M. The US Army reports that enemy ships are approaching southwest of Pearl Harbor. The reports, like many others following the attack, are false.

4.28 P.M. Search and rescue operations continue in Pearl Harbor. The *Arizona* suffered the most destruction. Japanese bombers scored four direct hits on the ship, and three devastating near misses. Of the 1,400 crewmen on board, 1,177 were killed in the explosions.

The *Arizona* sank. It still remains at the bottom of Pearl Harbor.

9.00 P.M. US bombers from the aircraft carrier *Enterprise* arrive at Oahu. US ground forces think the bombers are Japanese and fire at them. Fortunately, no one is injured. Americans are on edge and fearful of more attacks.

5.15 A.M. 8 December, 5.15 a.m. False reports and rumours continue to circulate. Hawaiian police report that Japanese parachute troops are landing in Kalihi Valley, east of Pearl Harbor. US forces are given orders to "shoot anything that moves".

The shallow waters of the harbour make it possible to raise several damaged ships and repair them.

Crewmen, civilian workers, divers, and other skilled workers from private companies tackle the repair jobs.

The attack on Pearl Harbor has not crippled the US fleet as badly as the Japanese had hoped.

Most of the damaged US ships are repaired and sent back into action. Within weeks, American troops would be fighting around the world.

CONCLUSION: WORLD WAR II

Throughout the 1930s, the United States had been growing increasingly concerned about Japan's aggressive expansion in the East. Japan had become the most powerful force in East Asia, but did not have the raw materials to support the demands of industry and its growing population. Japanese invasions of Manchuria and China caused considerable unease amongst the Western powers.

In an attempt to stop Japan's expansion, the United States imposed severe sanctions on oil and other resources. The United States demanded that Japan withdraw from China and abandon its expansion plans. Reliant on the United States for oil, Japan was forced to decide whether to accept the sanctions or go to war with the United States. It responded by attacking Pearl Harbor on 7 December 1941.

Before the attack on Pearl Harbor, most Americans opposed going to war with Japan. The attack, however, united the American people against a common enemy. Government, citizens, businesses, and industries jumped into action and prepared for war.

Japan, however, would not be alone in the conflict. On 11 December, Nazi Germany declared war on the United States. German leader Adolf Hitler had signed an agreement with Japan agreeing to support it in the event of war. The United States was now involved in a global conflict, fighting wars in the Pacific and in Europe.

The Americans got revenge on the Japanese six months later at the Battle of Midway. US aircraft flying from three carriers sunk four Japanese carriers and destroyed 250 Japanese planes. The American victory stopped the Japanese advance in the Pacific and turned the tide of the war.

On the home front, the US government and the American citizens began to distrust people of Japanese ancestry. The government set up war relocation camps, mostly in the West and Southwest. The camps were located in remote areas, often in hot and dry climates. Roughly 120,000 Japanese people were forced to live in the camps. About two-thirds of the people put into the camps were American citizens, and some ended up living in the camps for generations. Families were often split up and many people lost their homes and businesses.

By May 1945, Germany surrendered, ending the war in Europe. By that time, Japan was near defeat, but still fighting. In August, the United States dropped two newly developed atomic bombs on Japan, with devastating effect. Over 100,000 people were killed instantly, and many more would die later from radiation sickness. The bombs dealt a final blow to the Japanese war effort.

The war with Japan ended with Japan's surrender on the USS *Missouri* on 2 September 1945, in Tokyo Bay. But it all began on 7 December 1941, at Pearl Harbor.

TIMELINE

26 November 1941	A fleet of Japanese warships sets sail for Oahu, Hawaii, home of Pearl Harbor
7 December 1941	
3.42 a.m., Hawaiian time	The US minesweeper *Condor* spots the periscope of a Japanese mini-sub 3.2 kilometres (2 miles) from Pearl Harbor
6.15 a.m.	Vice Admiral Chuichi Nagumo sends Japanese aircraft to begin their attack
6.45 a.m.	The *Ward* fires depth charges and sinks the Japanese mini-submarine sighted by the *Condor*
7.02 a.m.	The Opana Mobile Radar Station spots Japanese planes above northern Oahu
7.49 a.m.	Commander Mitsuo Fuchida, flying over the island, gives his order to begin the attack
7.51 a.m.	Zeros strafe PBY Catalinas at Kaneohe Naval Air Station
7.53 a.m.	Attackers blast parked aircraft at Ewa Field
7.55 a.m.	Val dive-bombers strike Hickam Field; planes attack US vessels moored in Pearl Harbor
7.58 a.m.	Torpedoes explode into the *West Virginia* and the *Oklahoma*
8.00 a.m.	Torpedoes rip into the side of the *California*; the *Oklahoma* is hit again
8.06 a.m.	A bomb hits the forward magazine of the *Arizona*
8.10 a.m.	President Roosevelt is told of the attack
8.25 a.m.	At Schofield Barracks, Second Lieutenant Stephen Saltzman and Sergeant Lowell Klatt open fire on enemy aircraft
8.50 a.m.	In Washington DC, Secretary of State Hull meets with Japanese ambassador to the United States
9.05 a.m.	Planes from the second wave attack Wheeler Field
9.06 a.m.	Bombs strike the destroyers *Downes* and *Cassin* as they sit in dry dock

The times given in this book are approximate and may vary between sources.

9.30 a.m.	Three bombs hit the destroyer *Shaw*, which is moored in dry dock
9.50 a.m.	The *Blue* drops six depth charges and destroys a Japanese mini-sub
11.00 a.m.	Commander Fuchida assesses the damage the attack has caused
12.30 p.m.	Police and FBI agents in Honolulu, Hawaii, raid the Japanese embassy and discover Japanese officials destroying secret codebooks and important documents
1.00 p.m.	Vice Admiral Nagumo decides not to launch a third wave of attack
1.12 p.m.	More false reports are made claiming the enemy is attacking again
8 December, 6.30 a.m. Hawaiian time; 12.30 p.m. in Washington DC	President Roosevelt addresses Congress; he signs a declaration of war later in the day

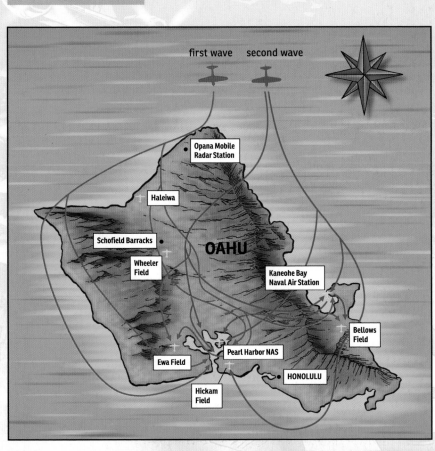

CAST OF CHARACTERS

Cordell Hull (1871–1955)
Hull was the US secretary of state from 1933 to 1944. Hull was responsible for US diplomatic relations with Japan before and during the attack on Pearl Harbor. He is called the "father of the United Nations" for his efforts to create and establish that international organization.

Franklin Delano Roosevelt (1882–1945)
Roosevelt was the 32nd president of the United States, and the president at the time of the Pearl Harbor attack. FDR, as he was commonly known, gave strong diplomatic and financial support to China and Great Britain in the early years of World War II (1939–1945). During the early years of the war, the United States remained officially neutral in the conflict. Roosevelt died in April 1945, several months before the war ended.

Admiral Isoroku Yamamoto (1884–1943)
Yamamoto was the commander in chief of the Combined Fleet, the main fighting force of the Imperial Japanese Navy. He was responsible for the development of naval aviation in the early years of the war and was the master planner of the attack on Pearl Harbor. He died when American fighter planes shot down his aircraft in a secretly planned ambush.

Vice Admiral Chuichi Nagumo (1887–1944)
Nagumo was commander in chief of the Imperial Japanese Navy's main aircraft carrier force. He was opposed to Admiral Yamamoto's plan to attack the US Navy at Pearl Harbor. He commanded the raid on Pearl Harbor, but was later criticized for not launching a third wave of attack planes. He committed suicide while attempting to defend the island of Saipan against a US assault.

Hirohito (1901–1989)

Hirohito was emperor of Japan during World War II. In the 1930s, he forged alliances with Germany and Italy, forming the Axis powers. Even when Japan was losing the war in the Pacific, he refused to surrender. Finally, after the atomic bombings of Hiroshima and Nagasaki and the Soviet declaration of war on Japan, Hirohito surrendered.

Mitsuo Fuchida (1902–1976)

Fuchida was a captain and a bomber pilot in the Imperial Japanese Navy during World War II. He led the first wave of air attacks on Pearl Harbor and was responsible for coordinating the entire raid under fleet commander Vice Admiral Nagumo.

George Welch (1918–1954) and Ken Taylor (1919–2006)

Welch and Taylor were second lieutenants and pilots stationed at Wheeler Field on the morning of the attack. They alerted nearby Haleiwa Field to quickly get two P-40 Tomahawk fighters ready for action. The pair drove to Haleiwa at high speed, manned their planes, and flew into combat. They shot down six planes, including two Vals and a Zero.

Doris "Dorie" Miller (1919–1943)

Miller was a cook in the US Navy serving aboard the battleship USS *West Virginia* when Japanese torpedoes struck it during the attack on Pearl Harbor. Miller manned an anti-aircraft machine gun and fired at attacking Japanese planes. He died at the Battle of Tarawa when a Japanese torpedo struck his ship.

GLOSSARY

aircraft carrier warship with a large, flat deck where aircraft take off and land

ambassador top person sent by a government to represent it in another country

barracks large building or group of buildings where soldiers are housed

battleships large armoured warships with heavy-calibre guns

bow front section of a ship or boat

civilians people who are not members of the armed forces

destroyer fast warship that travels with larger vessels and defends them against smaller, powerful attackers

light cruiser warship that is smaller than a battleship but larger than a destroyer

magazine part of a ship where ammunition is stored

moored when a boat is tied to a pier or anchor

periscope vertical tube containing mirrors and lenses that allows the user to see objects that would otherwise be hidden from sight. Submarines use periscopes to see above the water.

stern rear section of a ship or boat

strafe attack with machine gun fire from low-flying aircraft

torpedo underwater bomb shaped like a tube that explodes when it hits a target

FIND OUT MORE

Books

Captured Off Guard: The Attack on Pearl Harbor (Graphic Flash Graphic Novels), Donald Lemke (Stone Arch Books, 2008)

Pearl Harbor: Before And Beyond: The Eyewitness Account of Steve Rula, Steve Rula (AuthorHouse, 2012)

Pearl Harbor: The U.S. Enters World War II (24/7 Goes to War), Steve Dougherty (Franklin Watts, 2010)

World War II (Eyewitness) (Dorling Kindersley, 2012)

World War II in the Pacific: From Pearl Harbor to Nagasaki (The United States at War), R. Conrad Stein (Enslow Publishers, 2011)

DVDs

Attack on Pearl Harbor: A Day of Infamy (Quantum Leap, 2008)

Tora! Tora! Tora!: The Real Story of Pearl Harbour (History Channel, 2011)

Ultimate Collections: World War II: The War in Europe and the Pacific (History Channel, 2012)

Websites

www.eyewitnesstohistory.com/pearl.htm
Read a chilling firsthand account by a US Marine who survived the bombing of the USS *Arizona*.

www.history.navy.mil/photos/events/wwii-pac/pearlhbr/pearlhbr.htm
This site offers hundreds of photos documenting the attack, oral histories, survivor reports, and much more.

www.nps.gov/valr/index.htm
This site features articles, photos, videos, and oral history interviews about the attack on Pearl Harbor.

www.pbs.org/wgbh/nova/military/killer-subs-pearl-harbor.
html
Watch a full-length PBS documentary about an expedition to
locate and study Japanese mini-subs that sank during
the attack.

Place to visit

If you are ever in the United States, you could visit this historic
site in Honolulu, Hawaii.

Pacific Historic Parks – Pearl Harbor Visitor Center & USS
***Arizona* Memorial**
National Park Service
USS *Arizona* Memorial
1 Arizona Memorial Place
Honolulu, Hawaii 96818
808-422-3300
pacifichistoricparks.org

Tour the USS *Arizona* Memorial, built over the remains of the
sunken battleship, and sites on Ford Island, including the USS
Oklahoma Memorial and the USS *Utah* Memorial.

INDEX